RARE AND PRECIOUS
METALS

PLATINUM

By Greg Roza

Gareth Stevens
Publishing

Please visit our website, www.garethstevens.com. For a free color catalog of all our high-quality books, call toll free 1-800-542-2595 or fax 1-877-542-2596.

Library of Congress Cataloging-in-Publication Data

Roza, Greg.
Platinum / by Greg Roza.
 p. cm. — (Rare and precious metals)
Includes index.
ISBN 978-1-4824-0507-1 (pbk.)
ISBN 978-1-4824-0508-8 (6-pack)
ISBN 978-1-4824-0504-0 (library binding)
1. Platinum — Juvenile literature. I. Roza, Greg. II. Title.
QD181.P8 R69 2014
546.645—dc23
First Edition

Published in 2014 by
Gareth Stevens Publishing
111 East 14th Street, Suite 349
New York, NY 10003

Designer: Nicholas Domiano
Editor: Therese Shea

Photo credits: Cover, p. 1 optimarc/Shutterstock.com; Inset Graphic: Aleksandr Bryliaev/Shutterstock.com; Caption Box: Hemera/Thinkstock.com; text background, pp. 5, 7, 17 iStockphoto/Thinkstock.com; p. 9 Vitaly Korovin/Shutterstock.com; p. 11 Stephen Hilger/Bloomberg/Getty Images; p. 13 casadaphoto/Shutterstock.com; p. 15 Jasmin Awad/Shutterstock.com; p. 19 Stocktrek Images/Getty Images; p. 21 © iStockphoto.com/photosbyjim.

Printed in the United States of America

CPSIA compliance information: Batch #CW14GS: For further information contact Gareth Stevens, New York, New York at 1-800-542-2595.

Contents

Words in the glossary appear in **bold** type the first time they are used in the text.

Make the Most of Metals

Metals are elements found inside Earth—and all over the **universe**! Most are shiny when polished. They're good at carrying, or conducting, electricity and heat. Most metals are **malleable**, and some can be stretched into thin wires. Because of these qualities, metals are used to make cars, computers, toys, jewelry, and many other products.

Unlike metals such as iron and aluminum, platinum is very rare. This makes it very expensive. Platinum is highly prized for its metallic features.

METAL MANIA!

When music groups sell 1 million copies of an album in the United States, the album is said to "go platinum."

oxygen gas

liquid mercury

solid platinum

Elements—such as the gas oxygen, the liquid mercury, and the solid platinum—are kinds of matter that can't be broken down into other types of matter. There are more than 100 elements.

5

Get to Know Platinum

Platinum is one of the least reactive metals. That means it doesn't easily form **compounds**. Some metals, such as iron, easily join with oxygen in the air to form rust. However, platinum doesn't react with oxygen, so it doesn't rust. Platinum shines when polished. Also, it's malleable, so it can be hammered and bent into useful shapes.

Platinum has a high melting point: 3,216°F (1,769°C). Containers made of platinum, called crucibles, are used to hold the liquid form of metals that melt at lower temperatures.

METAL MANIA!

Platinum is **denser** than metals such as gold and silver. This quality makes platinum heavier than many other metals.

The least reactive metals, such as gold and platinum, are sometimes found in nature in pure forms called nuggets.

7

How Rare Is Rare?

Gold is rare, but platinum is rarer. It's been **estimated** that all the gold ever mined would fill three large swimming pools. Or, shaped into a cube, the gold would measure about 67 feet (20 m) on each side. All the platinum mined so far would fit inside a cube just 20 feet (6 m) long and 20 feet high.

Some people think there's more platinum than gold on Earth. Platinum is also more common in the universe. However, it's much harder to mine than gold. Platinum is still far rarer than metals such as iron and nickel.

METAL MANIA!

Platinum is the most common element of the "platinum group metals": ruthenium, rhodium, palladium, osmium, iridium, and platinum. These metals share similar features.

8

Platinum was once far more expensive than gold. However, the prices for the two metals have grown closer together. Sometimes gold is more expensive than platinum.

9

Unwanted?

More than 2,000 years ago, people in South America used platinum to make jewelry and decorations. Starting in the 1400s, Spanish adventurers came to South America in search of gold and silver. To them, platinum was worthless. They dumped an untold fortune of platinum in the sea while searching rivers for gold and silver.

In the mid-1700s, two Europeans each identified platinum as an element. Soon, people around the world realized how rare and valuable the metal really is.

METAL MANIA!

Around 700 BC, an Egyptian leader was buried in a box decorated with platinum. Today, the platinum is still shiny.

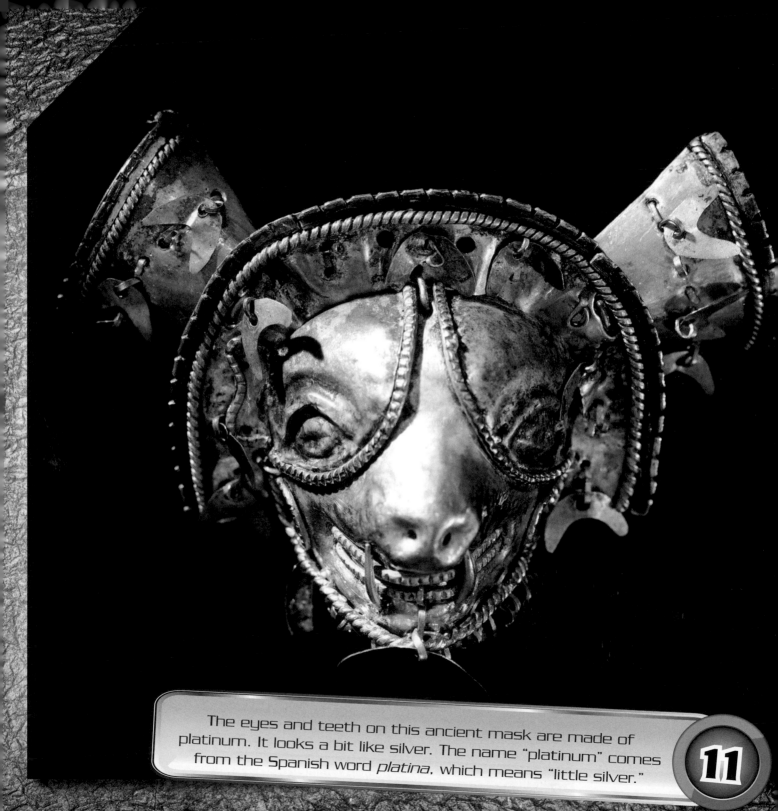

The eyes and teeth on this ancient mask are made of platinum. It looks a bit like silver. The name "platinum" comes from the Spanish word *platina*, which means "little silver."

11

Platinum Places

Pure platinum nuggets are sometimes found in nature, but platinum is also found in **minerals** such as sperrylite (SPEHR-ih-lyt) and cooperite. We call these minerals platinum ores, because they're an important source of the metal. The platinum group metals are often found together in **deposits** of nickel and copper.

South African mines produce the most platinum per year. In the Ural Mountains of Russia, platinum is collected from ore found in copper-nickel mines. Other important producers include Zimbabwe, Canada, the United States, and Colombia.

METAL MANIA!

When Earth was forming, all its platinum sunk to Earth's core, or center. Some scientists think the platinum we find today came from space rocks that hit Earth about 3.6 billion years ago.

Sperrylite is a mixture of the elements platinum and arsenic. Arsenic is very poisonous.

The Bushveld Complex

The Bushveld Complex in South Africa contains the world's largest deposits of platinum group metals. These elements are found in layers called reefs.

In some areas of the Bushveld Complex, open-pit mining is used. Large machines scrape away a layer of earth, the ore is removed, and then another layer is scraped away. Over time, this creates a large pit.

Some reefs are narrow and deep. Workers drill holes and fill them with **explosives**. After blasting the rocks, workers collect the ore.

METAL MANIA!

The Bushveld Complex formed about 2 billion years ago when melted rock inside Earth rose up through cracks and cooled. This is known as an intrusion.

Miners first began working at the Bushveld Complex looking for platinum in 1925. Today, mining companies still find platinum group metals and many other elements there.

15

Making Pure Platinum

Platinum ores contain more elements than just platinum. The elements are separated during a long, complex process called refining.

Platinum ore is crushed into a sand and mixed with water and **chemicals**. Air is passed through the mixture. Elements, including platinum group metals, bubble to the surface, where they're collected. This mixture is then heated in a special oven until it melts and the metals group together. Electricity and more chemicals are used to further separate the metals.

METAL MANIA!

Why is platinum so expensive? Up to 12 tons (10.9 mt) of ore must be refined to get just 31.1 grams—or about **1 troy ounce**—of pure platinum!

Smelting is the process of heating ore until it melts. The unwanted portion, known as slag, is poured off. The rest is cooled and formed into shapes.

17

Pretty and "Green"

Platinum has been used to make jewelry for hundreds of years. It shines when polished, doesn't rust, and it's **durable**.

In the 1800s, scientists discovered that platinum is a useful catalyst. A catalyst is a substance that causes or increases the speed of a chemical reaction without going through any changes itself. A common car part called a catalytic converter uses platinum to change harmful **exhaust** products into less harmful gases. Platinum helps keep our air safe to breathe!

METAL MANIA!

More than a third of platinum produced today is used to make catalytic converters.

The platinum in a catalytic converter changes, or converts, harmful gases into gases that aren't as bad for the world around us.

19

Platinum Alloys

An alloy is a solid mixture of two or more elements, at least one of which is a metal. These mixtures combine the strengths of different elements to make a metal that's even more useful.

Platinum and iridium alloys produce jewelry that's very shiny and doesn't get scratched easily. Alloys of platinum and ruthenium are hard to shape and not as shiny, but they're very durable. An alloy of platinum and the element cobalt is used to make powerful magnets.

diamonds mounted in platinum

The Many Uses of Platinum

jewelry

watches

decorations

catalytic converters

electronics

powerful magnets

medical tools

dental implants

cancer drugs

computer parts

crucibles

glass production

This chart lists even more uses for the rare and precious metal platinum.

Glossary

chemical: matter that can be mixed with other matter to cause changes

compound: matter that is a mixture of two or more elements

dense: packed very closely together

deposit: an amount of a mineral in the ground that built up over a period of time

durable: strong and able to resist wear

estimate: to make a careful guess about an answer based on the known facts

exhaust: waste gases created by a car's motor

explosive: something that can blow up or explode

malleable: able to be bent and shaped

mineral: matter in the ground that forms rocks

troy ounce: a unit of measurement used to weigh precious metals. A troy ounce equals 31.1 grams.

universe: everything that exists

For More Information

Books

Montgomerie, Adrienne. *Metals*. New York, NY: Crabtree Publishing, 2013.

Oxlade, Chris. *Rocks and Minerals*. Chicago, IL: Capstone Heinemann Library, 2014.

Wood, Ian. *Platinum*. New York, NY: Benchmark Books, 2004.

Websites

Periodic Table
www.ducksters.com/science/periodic_table.php
Learn more about platinum and all the other elements of the periodic table.

Platinum: The Essentials
www.webelements.com/platinum/
Read more facts about platinum.

Index